PATCHWORK

PATCHWORK

Mary Moody

Bloomsbury Books
London

Previous page: A sampler quilt designed by Susan Harris.

Acknowledgements:
Thanks to Susan Harris of Hearts and Hands; Jennie Kants and Di England of Wentworth Falls, Sydney.

Published by Harlaxton Publishing Ltd
2 Avenue Road, Grantham, Lincolnshire, NG31 6TA, United Kingdom.
A Member of the Weldon International Group of Companies.

First published in 1992.

This edition published in 1993 by
Bloomsbury Books
an imprint of
The Godfrey Cave Group
42 Bloomsbury Street, London. WC1B 3QJ
under license from Harlaxton Publishing Ltd.

Publishing Manager: Robin Burgess
Project Coordinator: Lynn Bryan
Project assistant: Jenny Johnson
Editor: Dulcie Andrews
Illustrator: Carol Ohlbach
Photographer: Andrew Elton
Designer: Kathie Baxter Smith
Produced in Singapore by Imago

British Library Cataloguing-in-Publication data.
A catalogue record for this book is available from the British Library.
Title: Country Crafts Series: Patchwork
ISBN:1 85471 116 4

CONTENTS

INTRODUCTION

The popularity of creating a beautiful piece of craft by hand is increasing among people of all age groups.

Through this Country Craft series, it is our hope that you will find satisfaction and enjoyment in learning a new skill. In this case, that of patchwork. The making of a patchwork piece brings joy both to the maker, the family and the lucky recipient of a finely crafted gift. For those who are practical, patchwork is easy to do once you know the method, as you will discover.

Opposite: Terracotta pots in a row feature in this lovely quilted patchwork wall-hanging.

HISTORY OF PATCHWORK

THE CRAFT OF PATCHWORK has been practised for centuries in many countries, but most notably in North America during the 19th century.

While there are examples of patchwork dating back to Egyptian times, the pieces most often remembered are the imaginative works of thrifty pioneer women.

These earlier examples of patchwork, mainly quilts and bedcovers, were made as a matter of economy and necessity, to recycle used or scrap fabrics and to provide essential warm covers where blankets were scarce. This was true for colonial settlers in North America who experienced long, harsh winters in remote parts of the country. Pioneer women worked individually and in groups, creating a rich history in cloth, a history which only today is being properly recognised and documented.

Patchwork also provided women with a creative and useful occupation during winter when they were trapped indoors for months at a time. Girls as young as three were taught needlework skills, and began making patchwork blocks under the watchful eyes of their mothers and grandmothers. Many had finished enough blocks for a quilt cover by their fifth birthday.

One of the reasons for the popularity of patchwork in North America was the booming cotton industry, made possible by the labour of slaves in the southern states. As printed cotton fabric became cheap, plentiful and pretty, women stopped making quilts just for economic reasons, and started to create masterpieces of design using fabric especially chosen for the task.

In contrast, early Australian settlers created far fewer examples of patchwork because the climate was so much milder and because wool was the main fabric industry – printed or plain cotton fabric was scarce and expensive. Even so, there are some excellent examples of patchwork and quilting crafted by pioneer Australian women, now on display in museums throughout Australia.

When the manufacturing industries emerged at the end of the last century, patchwork became less popular among housewives, who could now buy ready-made bedcovers and blankets cheaply. Quilting and patchwork fell from favour as these were considered slow and time-consuming chores.

However, since the 1970's, patchwork has enjoyed a revival, as both men and women look for satisfying and creative outlets to balance the hectic pace of modern life. Cotton fabrics are now designed and printed just for the patchwork market, with new designs, colours, and styles coming out every season.

Many patchworkers still use second-hand and recycled fabrics, while others prefer to select material specifically for each project, co-ordinating colour schemes to match interior decor.

The main block in this quilt is 'Dove in the window' a design dating back to 1898.

The scope for creating individual pieces is limitless. Country-style patchwork is extremely popular, the stitching together of floral prints, plaids, checks and plain fabrics in warm, pleasing combinations. Popular too are the Amish designs, featuring black fabric together with other plain colours, which can be very effective. Designs also give scope for individual creativity, from bold geometric designs to the old-fashioned sampler quilt.

As a hobby, making patchwork is satisfying and relaxing. Once the basic techniques are understood, the challenge to create valuable family heirlooms will encourage you to work steadily on your projects. Hand made quilts, although relatively inexpensive in material costs, are very costly to buy, and therefore make wonderful – and very personal – gifts for family and friends.

This Amish-style quilt made of taffeta, with a pleated trim, is by Jennie Kants.

TOOLS AND MATERIALS

ALTHOUGH PATCHWORK began as a low-cost method of recycling second-hand fabrics, as a modern-day hobby it can be very expensive. How much you spend, and how many different tools or gadgets you buy to make the activity faster and easier, will depend very much on your personal budget and commitment to the craft.

It is possible to work efficiently with just a ruler, pencil, and scissors. However, there is much more sophisticated equipment available at specialist patchwork or sewing shops, to make the measuring and cutting more accurate and certainly easier.

As a beginner it is best to start with the basics, and gradually build up a collection of useful equipment as you attempt more adventurous projects.

THE BASICS

Needles Good quality needles are essential. Try to use the finest needles possible, to get a finer finish on your work. For patchwork piecing 'between' needles are required, although if a longer needle is preferred, use 'sharps' from No. 7 to No. 10. Fine needles are difficult to thread, and a needle-threader may also be a good investment to save frustration.

Thread Fine cotton thread has always been used for patchwork; however some of the newer polyester core-wrapped threads are fine. Even so they have a tendency to knot or fray, and this can be avoided by only using a short piece at a time (no more than 30cm [12 inches]) and by always threading the needle with the freshly cut end. Use a light colour when sewing light patches and a dark colour when sewing darker patches. When sewing a light patch to a dark patch, use a darker thread, which will make the stitches less apparent.

Pins Glass- or plastic-headed pins are fine and therefore good for holding fabrics together; however sturdier pins are needed to pin fabric to cardboard templates (see Template).

Thimbles Although many modern sewers are unaccustomed to sewing with thimbles, they are essential for the quilting process, and also for basic patchwork. Metal, plastic or leather thimbles will do, and there are special thimbles to protect thumbs as well as your fingers.

Scissors Good, sharp scissors make a marked difference to the accuracy of cutting. If possible, buy good quality scissors and keep them aside, only to be used for cutting fabric. Have separate scissors for cutting cardboard templates. If you live in a family where scissors are borrowed for school projects, buy inexpensive ones that can be replaced

Opposite: A single patch scrap quilt by Olga Rumble.

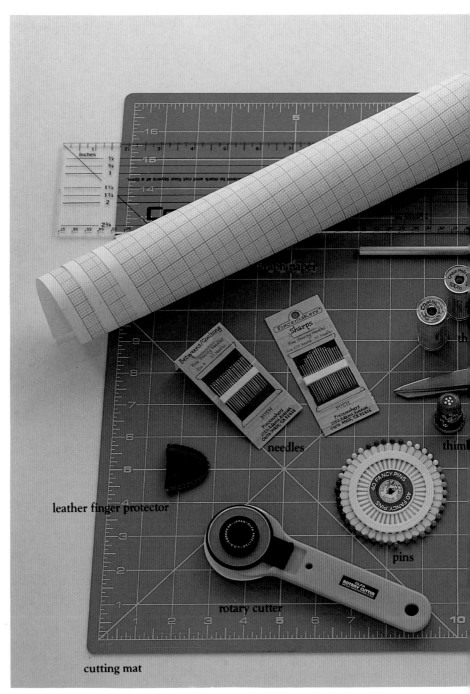

needles

thim[

leather finger protector

pins

rotary cutter

cutting mat

clear plastic ruler

pencils

scissors

templates

sewing basket

economically.

Rulers   A clear plastic ruler, the wider the better, will improve the accuracy in measuring and ruling templates and fabric. One problem is that designs can be given in either metric or imperial measures, and a ruler that shows both is more useful. Specialist patchwork shops have many rulers designed for the purpose and, although these are sometimes expensive, they are a worthwhile investment for the sake of accuracy.

Pencils   Whether using a soft lead pencil or fabric marker, remember to keep it sharp for a fine, accurate line. Marking pens that fade after several hours are also useful.

Graph paper   This is used when altering the size of templates or creating new designs. These can be copied onto graph paper from a book, then enlarged or reduced, using a photocopying machine.

Templates   Templates are shapes of thin cardboard, plastic or metal used as a guide in cutting and available in a wide range of sizes. Each set has a large and small template – the large one is for cutting the fabric and the small one indicates the actual size of the patch. It is cheaper to cut your own templates in cardboard using patterns from books or magazines.

OPTIONAL EXTRAS

Cutting mat   There are many sizes and shapes of rubber mats, some with a grid incorporated, for measuring and cutting fabric. These are excellent for large-scale projects, where fast cutting is important.

Rotary cutters   These are sharp, accurate cutting blades in a plastic handle, and again they are ideal when cutting large quantities of fabric.

Quilter's quarter This is a clear plastic rule used for making seam allowances around templates.

Storage baskets or shelves   To keep fabric clean and organised while the work is in progress. Keen quilters sometimes have an entire cupboard set aside for storing the fabrics and equipment needed for the craft.

The fabrics   Firmly woven, lightweight, pure cotton is the preferred material for making patchwork. Although polyester cotton blends are also manageable they should have at least 50 per cent cotton content.

Specialist fabric shops generally stock cotton patchwork fabric but, if you are uncertain, check on the bolt for the fabric composition. Scrap quilts can be made from any left-over cotton fabric, but try to choose materials of the same weight to give a smooth finish. Experienced hands can experiment with velvets and silks for special projects, but beginners should use cotton which is much easier to handle and sew.

Opposite: A machine sewn patchwork cushion using the 'Log Cabin' design.
Following page: Detail of a patch of a 'Log Cabin' quilt by Margaret Ross.

STARTING WORK

PATCHWORK is a distinctive personal craft with unlimited scope for individual creativity and expression in terms of design, style, and use of fabric colour and texture. The traditions of design and use of fabric go back for centuries.

Many people love the old-fashioned look of traditional North American patchwork style, while others prefer a more modern look, or crazy patchwork, where form and style are only confined by imagination.

At first it is useful to study books to get a few ideas about designs, or perhaps attend a class on patchwork to gain basic knowledge of the techniques involved. From that point, your creative expression will emerge, encouraging experimentation with combinations of colour and designs.

Fabrics While we have touched on a few 'dos' and 'do nots' in fabric selection (see 'Tools and Materials'), there are many more factors to be considered. It is easy for new patchworkers to feel overawed at the array of fabrics available for the craft, and making a choice of colours and patterns for your first project can be quite daunting. However, it is interesting to see how well most fabrics look when patched together, and it is difficult to make a major error. It is really a matter of 'anything goes'. Country quilts look marvellous with the whole colour spectrum included; monochromatic schemes are also

effective, using the same basic colour in a variety of designs. The plain, bold colours of an Amish quilt, featuring a lot of black and primary colours, are also popular.

To begin with, try choosing three colours that work well together, then select fabrics in each colour that are both light and dark, patterned and plain. This should provide enough scope for a variety of interesting combinations.

CHOOSING FABRICS

Pattern: Select medium and small designs rather than those that are bold or wishy-washy, and will be lost when cut out and patched. Florals, checks, plaids or patterns with stripes or borders are all acceptable. Avoid fabrics with too much contrast between light and dark in the pattern (for example, black and white spots or stripes) as these will dominate and overpower other patterned fabrics.

Plain: Plain fabrics are necessary to help give the design definition, and to make the patterned fabrics show up more clearly. Choose from muted tones to bright primary colours, depending on the project.

Light or dark: Even a pastel quilt or cushion needs the emphasis of both lighter and darker shades and tones to strengthen the line of the pattern.

A pattern of hearts on a pink country-style fabric background makes an attractive cushion.

FABRIC SCRAPS

Although many people think that patchwork is made from discarded clothing or leftover scraps from other sewing projects, even early quilters combined scraps with materials that were bought specifically for the project in hand. Good quality cotton fabric scraps are great for your patchwork box and they add variety, colour, and interest to the finished work. One idea is to collect scraps from your children's clothes as they grow out of them or wear them out. Eventually you should have enough to make a scrap quilt that will be filled with memories of their childhood years.

DESIGN

The choice of design for a patchwork piece – whether it is a quilt or cushion – is personal. Designs vary radically, from geometrical traditional to modern pieces, to country-style sampler blocks, to appliqué, or crazy patchwork.

Most quilts, for example, are made from a series of blocks that are pieced individually, then joined together to form the top layer of the quilt. A sampler quilt features a series of blocks in different designs, often using the same fabrics, which are then joined together with strips of another fabric (called lattice). However, there are thousands of other ways of combining blocks to form an overall design, such as the standard 'log cabin' quilt or the 'tumbling blocks' quilt.

Beginners should practise simple designs and graduate to more complex patterns as skill and confidence increases.

This design is called 'Necktie' and was first seen in North America in 1898.

When combining fabrics in either blocks, or to form an overall design, there are some basic rules to follow which ensure the design is clearly defined.

Firstly, ensure there is a good balance of light, medium, and dark fabrics, and combine these so that two dark fabrics are not sewn side by side, or two light fabrics placed together. This is critical when geometric patterns are used or the designs will not stand out. Also try to achieve a good balance in the scale of the prints on the fabrics. Place large and small scale prints side by side, rather than combining two large or two small prints together in one block.

PATTERNS

The sources of quilt patterns is varied. Many of the blocks and designs commonly used today are based on those from North American colonial times. Most quilting books carry a range of designs which can be easily copied using graph paper and tracing paper. More simple patterns that rely on standard templates (hexagon, diamond, or triangle shapes) can also be easily adapted from books. If you are making your own cardboard templates, store them carefully in a paper bag, along with a graph of the design, for use another time. It is also possible to graph your own design following the basic instructions given in the next chapter.

GLOSSARY

Quilters and patchworkers speak their own language which can be confusing for beginners. This list will help you understand the meaning of each term.

Appliqué A technique of layering one or more fabrics on top of a larger square of fabric, creating a design

Block A single square of patchwork, pieced together either by hand or machine

Border The lattice around the edge of the quilt which can either be a strip of fabric (usually the same as the rest of the lattice), or strips of pieced patchwork

Lattice The fabric strips used to assemble, or set the blocks together. Sometimes also called 'sashing'

Piecing The process of sewing together the patchwork pieces. Which can be done either by hand or machine

Quilt top The finished patchwork after assembly, forming the top layer of the quilt

Quilting The process of joining quilt top, wadding, and backing fabric together to make a patchwork quilt.

A small running stitch is used template the cardboard or metal shape used as a pattern for cutting out the fabric

Template The cardboard or metal shape used as a pattern for cutting out the fabric.

Tying A method used instead of quilting, to hold three layers together

Opposite: A hand-dyed calico quilt designed by Jennie Kants.

*Called 'Trip Around The World' this is a beautiful example of an American antique quilt.
From Di England's private collection.*

TECHNIQUES OF THE CRAFT

THE MOST EXCITING ASPECT of making patchwork is choosing the design and selecting the fabrics. This is the initial, creative part of the project, and once this is completed the work begins in earnest.

In all stages of production accuracy is vital to success. Care must be taken with the drawing up of the pattern, the cutting of the templates, the cutting of the fabric and the sewing, or the patches simply will not fit together neatly, giving the finished work an untidy appearance.

TWO TECHNIQUES

Method One   This technique involves cutting out each shape, then tacking the fabric onto the cardboard templates for hand piecing. Piecing this way ensures clean lines and greater accuracy, as each piece is held rigid by the cardboard during the sewing process (see Fig. 1).

Method Two   This technique involves cutting the fabric out and marking the shape on the back of each piece, either for hand or machine piecing.

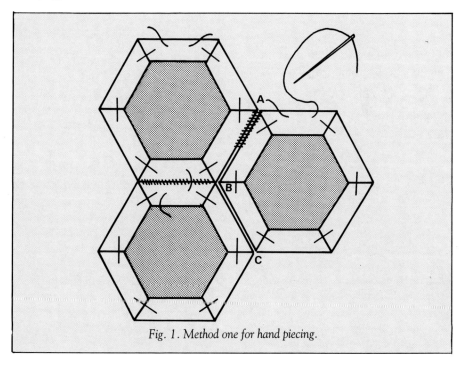

Fig. 1. Method one for hand piecing.

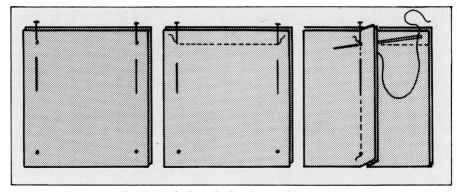

Fig. 2. Method two for hand or machine piecing.

Although the latter is faster, because the step of tacking onto cardboard templates is eliminated, great care must be taken to make sure the corners and edges meet exactly as marked on the fabric (see Fig. 2).

For both methods you will need a pattern or template.

DRAFTING A PATTERN

Whether you are making a small cushion or a large scale quilt, a pattern will be necessary. These are either in blocks (squares that are later joined together) or a repeated design, which is made in sections.

Each block can be broken down into shapes, according to the design. A block with four sections of design is called a four-patch (see Fig. 3), and there are also five-patch, seven-patch, and nine-patch designs.

Being able to break a block down into squares like this helps to simplify the drafting of a pattern.

Beginners should always start with a simple pattern that is either based on a ready-made metal or plastic template, or one that can be easily drafted using graph paper for a design from a book of patterns, as follows:

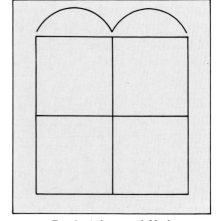

Fig. 3. A four-patch block.

1. Using tracing paper, carefully trace the design you like, then transfer it directly onto graph paper.

2. Generally the design will be much smaller than you require. Using a second sheet of paper draw up a grid, of the same size as the relevant block.

3. Now redraw the block design, following the lines on the enlarged grid. The design can be made as large or small as you wish by simply making the new grid larger or smaller.

28

The design transferred to graph paper and coloured to give an idea of how it will look when completed.

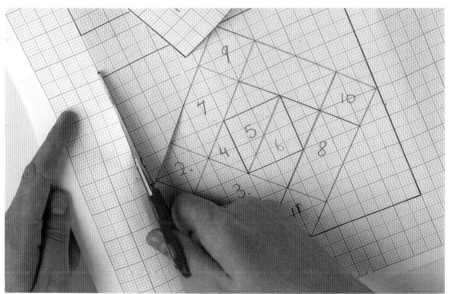

Number each segment of the pattern to help you identify each piece when cutting out the fabric.

This design forms the basis of the pattern to be made, with each repeat of the design becoming a section of the pattern.

4. Carefully number each piece of the pattern. This will help to match the numbers to the fabric required when cutting out. If you cannot easily visualise how the finished block will look, use the graph paper as a colouring-in sheet. Fill in the pattern in different colour combinations to see how the finished block will look.

Once you have the basic pattern it can then be used to cut out the cardboard templates.

Rather than cutting out templates as you go, spend an afternoon getting all the templates you need cut out in advance using paper or cardboard scissors (never use fabric scissors as they will become blunt). Making the templates at the same time avoids the stop and-start method which can slow down production. Always draw the design accurately, using a very sharp marking pencil to get a clean, straight line.

Handy tip

Do not spend money on sheet cardboard. Save empty cereal packets or Christmas cards from which you can make excellent templates.

WASH ALL FABRICS

It is a vital first step to wash all new fabrics before cutting begins. Some fabrics shrink and the colours in others may run. Imagine the dismay of spending months on a project, only to have it shrink or the dark colours run into the light fabrics after the first wash. Washing also removes fabric dressing which makes sewing difficult.

Wash each fabric separately in hot soapy water, then rinse it in hot water. Follow this by a final rinse in cold water. Dry the fabric either on the clothes line or in a clothes drier, then iron it smooth.

CUTTING THE FABRIC

Cutting with care will ensure that you get the most out of each piece of cloth. It is important, however, to understand how the cloth is woven, to give each block more stability.

Templates should be placed on the back of the fabric so that the largest side is running along the straight grain. Square and rectangular shapes are therefore placed so that the edge is in line with the straight grain, and triangles are positioned with the longest side of the template placed along the straight grain (see Fig. 4).

This way of cutting out templates is used to avoid buckling or stretching of pieces, which can easily happen if they are cut on the bias.

The selvage (the woven edge of the fabric) should always be removed when cutting the fabric.

If you are using a ready-made template with a matching window template, use the window template as the guide for accurate cutting out of the shape (see Fig. 5). If using a cardboard template onto which the fabric will then be tacked, pin the cardboard to the fabric and use a quilter's quarter to draw a cutting line.

HAND PIECING

Both of the above methods can be used for hand piecing.

If you are using cardboard templates, first tack the fabric onto the cardboard, ensuring all corners are neatly folded and finished (see

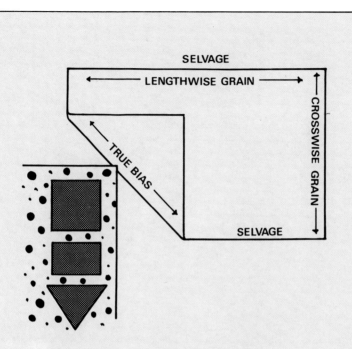

Fig. 4. Placing the template along the straight grain.

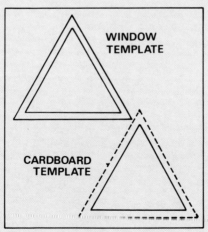

Fig. 5. Two types of template.

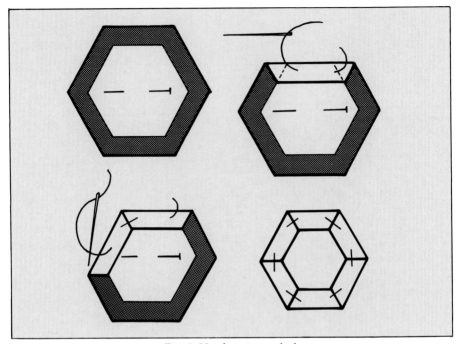

Fig. 6. Hand piecing methods.

Fig. 6). Hold two patches together, making sure that the two edges to be seamed are matched exactly, then join by over-sewing on the wrong side, using small, even stitches.

Stitches should be neat and firm, but not too tight. Do not knot the end of the cotton when piecing, but carefully over-stitch at the beginning of the join until the cotton is firm. Knots can be felt through a completed piece of patchwork.

If hand piecing without using templates, carefully mark the guide lines with a sharp marker pen or pencil. Pin two pieces of fabric together carefully before sewing them, and use a pin to make sure the marked corners meet exactly. Sew the pieces together using a neat, small running stitch. Check that the tension is firm but not too tight, and remember that any sections of loose stitches will show when the work is reversed. Do not knot the cotton at the beginning of a seam.

MACHINE SEWING

Machine sewing is faster but it is sometimes not as accurate as hand piecing. Many patterns, such as 'log cabin' are suitable for machine sewing, and there are methods for constructing a quilt in assembly-line fashion; however, this should only be done by experienced patchworkers.

Some quilts combine both hand and machine piecing. Generally the blocks are pieced by hand, then the lattice and borders are sewn on with a machine, as this requires

Hexagonel patches tacked onto cardboard and hand-stitched in the English style.

long, straight seams.

However, if you are piecing blocks with a machine, remember that accuracy is most important. Only *Method Two* is suited to machine sewing, and each seam should be pinned in place before you sew. Always sew exactly on the marked line and take care to finish each seam to prevent threads pulling.

If you are making a large patchwork top for a quilt, it is much easier to work in sections than to try to construct the entire top in one piece. This will be no problem if you are making individual blocks to be joined at the end with lattice strips. However, for an overall pattern like a hexagonal quilt, make the sections in a manageable size and then join these together to form the completed quilt top.

APPLIQUÉ

This is a popular method of making patchwork blocks or quilt tops. It involves cutting shapes and applying them to a background fabric to form a design.

To make appliqué, a pattern must be used. You can draft your own.

STEP-BY-STEP APPLIQUÉ

- Cut a cardboard template in the desired design
- Place the design on the back of the fabric and pin in place
- Cut around the shape, allowing a 5mm (1/4 in) seam
- Tack the fabric carefully to the cardboard, cutting around corners to avoid buckling
- Iron the shape carefully, to give a crisp outline seam
- Position on the background with care, using a pin to hold the shape in place
- Appliqué to the background fabric. The thread should match the darker of the two fabrics. Make a small knot in the end of the thread and bring it up into the folded edge of the appliqué piece. Pass the needle down through the background fabric, directly behind where the needle came up. Continue stitching around the shape in small stitches

Opposite: A machine sewn patchwork tea cosy.

FINISHING TECHNIQUES

AS EACH BLOCK or section of patchwork is completed it should be ironed carefully and stored flat until ready for assembly. If you are using *Method One* (in the previous chapter), you will need to remove the cardboard before ironing the fabric. However, when making a large quilt it is a good idea to leave the cardboard in while the block or section is stored.

To remove the cardboard use small scissors or a thread unpicker to cut the tacking stitch from the top side. Unpick all tacking thread, taking care to remove all the knotted ends, then fold back the seam and lift out the cardboard template.

If the cardboard has been treated carefully it can be reused several times, so store pieces together in a paper bag.

When ironing each block take care, making sure that the fabric does not stretch or buckle (this should not occur if the fabric has been cut out correctly along the straight grain). Seams should be pressed to one side, rather than pressed open, as this gives more stability

ASSEMBLING A QUILT TOP
Although most beginners start with a cushion or other small project, it is possible to graduate quickly to making a quilt – from a small quilt cover for a baby's cot to a more ambitious

king-sized bed quilt.

Some quilt tops are made by joining each block together to form a specific pattern, while in others the blocks are set into a frame of lattice strips (see Fig. 7).

The width of the lattice strips should be in proportion to the size of the blocks, and this can be estimated by closely examining an example of a finished quilt.

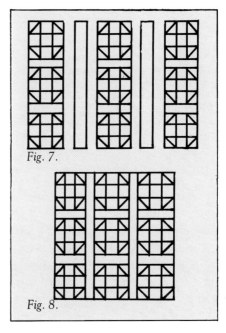

Fig. 7.

Fig. 8.

Opposite: A magnificent example of an American antique Crazy Patchwork quilt, dated 1923. From Di England's private collection.

37

If you have pre-designed your quilt on graph paper, also mark in the lattice to show the finished effect. In general, the lattice strips should be about one-third the width of the block (for example, if the block is 30cm [12 inches] square, the lattice strips should be 10cm [4 inches] wide). Do not forget to add on the 5mm [1/4 inch] seam allowance.

Lattice strips can be machine sewn, following the pattern in Fig. 8.

When the entire quilt top is assembled it should be ironed, with care, for the last time.

Iron all the seams to one side, making sure that the light seams are ironed under the darker fabric so these do not show through.

QUILTING OR TYING

A patchwork quilt is not simply a piece of patchwork sewn to a backing fabric – it must have a layer of wadding or filling to give it warmth, and to show the quilting stitches effectively. You can buy man-made, cotton or woollen wadding, which is available in various widths and can be brought cut to the length required.

Before quilting, lay the backing fabric (which should be slightly larger than the quilt top) on a large table or on the floor, right side down.

Cover this with the layer of wadding, then top with the patchwork, right side upwards. Spend some time adjusting the three layers so that they sit together smoothly and quite straight (see Fig. 9). Pin the layers together, starting from the centre and working outwards. Then tack the layers together with care, keeping in mind that a neat finish will make the quilting easier.

Quilting should be done in small sections, using a quilting frame to keep the layers smooth and taut. Always start in the centre of the quilt and work outwards.

The actual quilting stitch is simply a small, neat running stitch, but it takes time and patience to perfect it. Always use a small quilting needle and special quilting thread, and wear a thimble to push the needle through the layers. Also wear some form of protection on the finger that is used underneath as a pressure point for pushing the needle back up through the fabric.

Knot the end of the quilting thread and gently pull this knot through the fabric into the wadding from underneath. Then start the row of quilting.

Quilting designs and methods are discussed in more detail in the series companion book, *Quilting*.

Tying is simply a method of binding the three layers of the quilt together without actually quilting. It is described in detail in the 'Beginner's Project'.

QUILT EDGING

After quilting, the work should be finished with a rolled edging of bias fabric. The folded bias fabric can be machine sewn to the top of the quilt, then rolled over and hand sewn underneath.

CARE OF YOUR QUILT

Never store a quilt in a plastic bag or it may become mouldy. Quilts can be carefully machine washed on a delicate cycle using pure soap, then rinsed and lightly spin-dried. Lay out flat to dry, on an old sheet spread on the ground, never leaving the quilt top exposed to the hot sun for any length of time. With a little care your hand-crafted patchwork quilt should last several lifetimes.

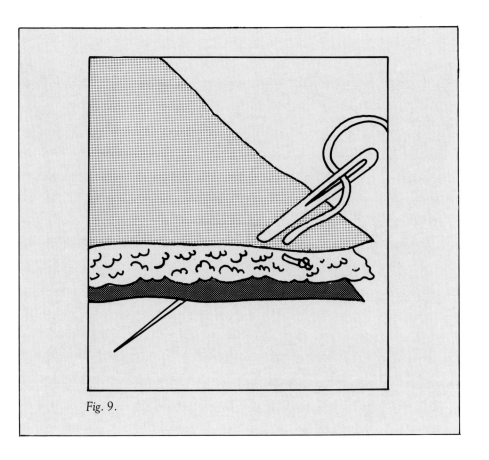

Fig. 9.

BEGINNER'S PROJECT

COUNTRY HEARTS CUSHION
Designed by Susan Harris

THIS CHARMING COUNTRY-STYLE cushion is an easy beginner's project, combining hand piecing, appliqué, quilting, and tying techniques. The patchwork itself is a block, made from four squares – two are simple nine-patch squares; two are squares of plain appliqué with floral hearts. The outline of the hearts is defined with a row of neat quilting, and the corners are held in place with ties. The patchwork top is then sewn to the backing fabric, opening down the back so the cushion can be removed and the cushion cover can be washed.

MATERIALS
Ruler, pencil or fabric marker, needles, thread to match fabric, cardboard for templates, scissors, cushion insert, button.

FABRIC
50cm (20 inches) checked fabric for nine-patch, and for backing the cushion
30cm (12 inches) plain fabric
20cm (8 inches) floral fabric
20cm (8 inches) fabric for borders
50cm (20 inches) fine lining (e.g. lawn)
50cm (20 inches) square of wadding

USEFUL HINTS
- Pure cotton fabric is best for patchwork
- Prewash all fabrics, rinse them well, dry and iron them
- Place templates on the wrong side of the fabric
- Trace templates onto fabric with a soft pencil or wash-out fabric marker

STEP ONE

Nine-patch (make 2) (see Fig. 1)
a) Carefully cut a 5cm (2 inch) square template from cardboard.
b) Place the template on the wrong side of the checked fabric and trace around it, allowing enough space between the pieces for a 5mm (1/4 inch) seam allowance. The pencil lines are the sewing lines, so cut along the seam allowance lines.
    Cut ten from the check fabric.
    Cut eight from the plain fabric.
c) To sew the nine-patch, place two right sides together (one check, one plain) and match the corners and seam lines with pins. Using a small back-stitch to begin with, sew from corner A to corner B (see Fig. 2).
d) Sew three strips of these (see Fig. 3).
e) Join the rows together, being careful to match the seams and not to sew over the seam allowances. Pass the needle to the other side, as this allows you to press the seams to the darker side.

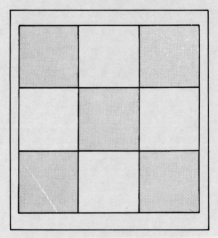

Fig. 1.

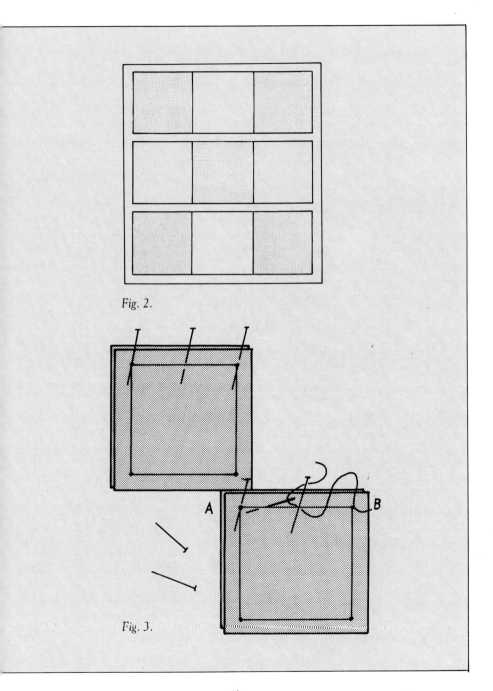

Fig. 2.

Fig. 3.

A

B

STEP TWO
Appliqué hearts (make 2)
a) Make a 15cm (6 inch) square template (see Fig. 4).
b) Trace around the template on the wrong side of the plain fabric, adding a 5mm (1/4 inch) seam allowance before cutting. Cut two of these squares.
c) Trace around the heart-shape and transfer this to cardboard. Two cardboard hearts will be needed.

Fig. 4.

d) Pin the heart-shapes to the wrong side of the floral fabric and cut out, allowing a 5mm (1/4 inch) seam allowance (see Fig. 5).

e) Tack the fabric to the cardboard heart-shape, clipping the fabric on the curves (see Fig. 6). Remove the pin and iron the fabric smooth on the wrong side to create a neat edge seam. After ironing well, remove the cardboard.

f) Place the heart in the centre of the plain square and tack it into place.

g) Appliqué all around the heart, using extra stitches in the centre curve.

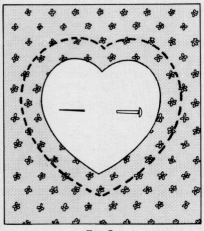

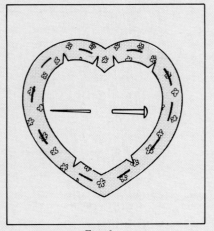

Fig. 5.   Fig. 6.

From the border fabric cut:

Two strips 6cm x 31 cm (2 1/4 x 12 1/4 inches).
Two strips 6cm x 41cm (2 1/4 x 16 inches).
Sew the short strips to the opposite side of the fabric,
then sew the longer strips to the top and bottom.

STEP THREE

Quilting cushion top

a) Layer the fine lining, wadding, and patchwork top together.

b) Tack the three layers, beginning in the middle and working out to the corners.

c) With a small quilting needle and quilting thread that matches the background fabric. With a fine running stitch to outline the heart.

STEP FOUR
Assembling the cushion top
Join the nine-patches to the appliqué patches, taking care to match the corners perfectly (see Fig. 7).

Fig. 7.

STEP FIVE
Tying the corners
a) Using six strands of embroidery thread, start from the right and go down into the back, then up clog to where the needle went in. Repeat the loop (see Fig. 8) then tie a double knot.
b) Cut thread about 5mm (1/4 inch) from knot.

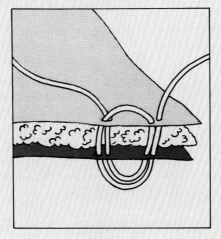

Fig. 8.

STEP SIX
Finishing the cushion
a) Cut two pieces of backing fabric, each 42 x 30cm (16 1/2 x 12 inches).
b) Hem along the side of each piece, making a buttonhole in the centre of one, and sewing a button onto the other.
c) Place the backing, right side up, on a flat surface. Then place the top, right side down on the backing. Pin all around, then sew a 5mm (1/4 inch) seam all around.
d) Trim and turn the right side out.
e) Fill with a 40 - 45cm (15 3/4 - 18 inch) cushion pad.

INDEX